*Portrait of*
# CALIFORNIA

 Portrait of America Series

# Portrait of CALIFORNIA

Photography by Ray Atkeson
Text by Lee Foster

**GRAPHIC ARTS CENTER PUBLISHING COMPANY**
Portland, Oregon

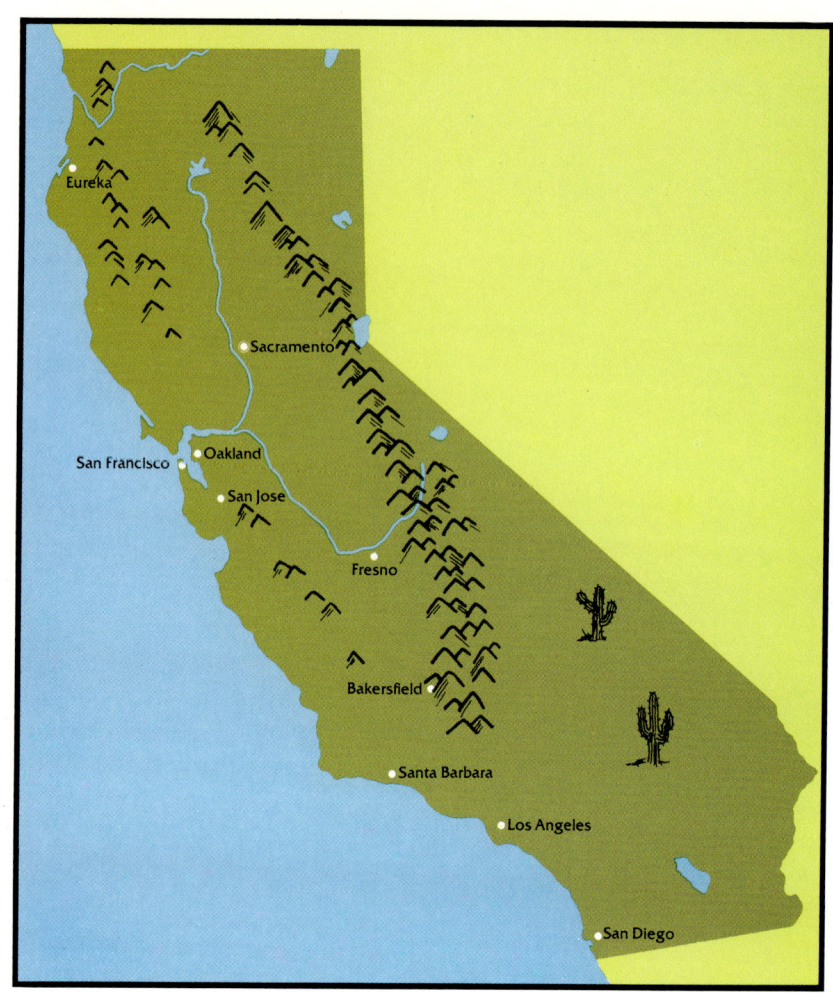

*Cover: Bridalveil Fall plunges 620 feet into Yosemite Valley, creating a rainbow in its mist as spring runoff swells all of Yosemite's waterfalls.*

*Title Page: The waters of San Luis Reservoir, part of the state's massive water project, are rippled by a summer breeze that wafts down from Pacheco Pass in the Diablo Range.*

International Standard Book Number 0-912856-54-8
Library of Congress catalog number 79-55978
Copyright© 1980 by Graphic Arts Center Publishing Company
2000 N.W. Wilson, Portland, Oregon 97209
Typesetting • Paul O. Giesey/Adcrafters
Printing • Graphic Arts Center
Binding • Lincoln & Allen
Printed in the United States of America

# Contents

SECTION I
*The Coast*

SECTION II
*The Sierra Nevada*

SECTION III
*The Valleys*

SECTION IV
*The Deserts*

# The Coast

The three-ton bull elephant seal opened his sleepy eyes and watched fearlessly as a ranger at Ano Nuevo State Park led our group of visitors within 20 feet of his sprawling body. Beyond the bull lay a cluster of 30 smaller, female seals, several nursing pups in January, preparing the offspring for the nine months of the year they would live in the open sea. I knew that next year, in the same December through February months, I could return to foggy Ano Nuevo, 70 miles south of San Francisco, and witness the primordial birthing and mating of these largest members of the pinniped family.

The story of the elephant seals parallels closely the larger tale of the California coast. Both seals and coast have an exquisite wild beauty and grandeur. Both were also endangered, the seals pushed close to extinction and the coast threatened with mindless development. And both are now protected for future generations.

In encounters with the elephant seals I have been impressed with their size, power, and relative indifference to mere man. Perhaps similar thoughts ran through the mind of the first white man who saw the California coast, Juan Rodríguez Cabrillo, a Portuguese navigator, when he explored this uncharted land of New Spain. On September 28, 1542, Cabrillo landed two vessels, the *San Salvador* and the *Victoria*, in a "port, closed and very good," the present San Diego harbor. At the Cabrillo National Monument on Point Loma, you can relive this moment of discovery.

When a traveler asks me, "Where is the best place to appreciate the full grandeur of the California coast?" I recommend Point Lobos State Reserve, south of Carmel. Each time I visit Point Lobos new pleasures of nature present themselves. In winter rafts of black brant geese float in the surf that pounds the jagged rock formations. The spring wildflowers include some less common varieties, such as golden blazing star. During summer divers with their wet suits and snorkels swim through an underwater trail in the kelp beds, occasionally coming nose to nose with sea otters. When the cold winds of autumn blow with force, gowen and Monterey cypress trees, crouched in deflective postures, become models of tenacity and perseverance.

At Muir Woods north of San Francisco and along Highway 101 from Sonoma County to the Oregon border lie parks that celebrate the coast redwood, *Sequoia sempervirens*, the tallest tree on the earth. Redwoods also persist farther south, such as at Pfeiffer–Big Sur and Big Basin parks, but the primary redwood country extends north from San Francisco. Virtues of the redwood as lumber include its unsurpassed durability when faced with the elements, its resistance to both water rot and termites, its large size, economical to harvest, its ease of sawing, and an appealing, reddish beauty when freshly cut that weathers to a silvery gray.

For the person who responds to nature, a grove of redwoods approximates the cathedral splendor that Chartres holds for the pious. Delicacy of the thin pinnate leaves, cones subtly small compared with showier pine cones, massive dimensions of the trees, the tendency to grow from sucker roots in tightly clustered families, hushed sunless ancient domains with thick carpets of needles, and clumps of lovely blue sorrel flowers are impressions I've carried from redwood country. My favorite viewing site is Founder's Grove in Humboldt Redwoods State Park. If you camp or picnic, go to nearby Albee Park, where on autumn evenings herds of deer will join you to harvest apples in the abandoned orchards of early pioneers.

The wild beauty of elephant seals, Point Lobos, and redwoods would have persisted untouched if the white man had never arrived. California Indians along the coast had neither the will nor the technology to dominate the environment. Elephant seals were too dangerous a quarry for their stone-tipped spears and arrows. Acorns, deer, fish, wild berries, and seeds were a more accessible diet. So the elephant seals lived peacefully for thousands of years until the Indian culture ended, within 50 years after the first Spanish missionaries arrived at San Diego in 1769. Regardless of the intentions of the Europeans, the fatal microbes of smallpox and tuberculosis doomed the Indians.

Two sites give you a good sense of the coast Indians.

At Carpinteria State Beach, south of Santa Barbara, you can walk along the sand and come upon large black banks of hardened tar, one of 13 natural oil seeps in the Santa Barbara Channel. Imaginative Chumash Indians, often considered the most advanced California tribe, used the sticky tar to caulk boards in their large, oceangoing canoes. Chumash were the only Indians in the United States with

*Left: Boats bask in the late afternoon sun at the Santa Barbara marina while rain falls in the Santa Ynez Mountains beyond.*

board boats. Spanish settlers marveled at Chumash skills and named the place La Carpinteria ("The Carpentry").

Kule Loklo is a re-created Coast Miwok Indian village at Point Reyes National Seashore. Coast Miwok life had some elements of an idyll: Food supplies were abundant, with plenty of acorns, seafood, and wild game. The population was a comfortable size. Climate was benign. Miwoks tended to die, not in wars—for which they had no word—but as a result of infections that developed after their teeth were worn down. At Kule Loklo you can see how the Miwok made bark teepees, wove reed baskets, cured animal skins, and leached the bitter tannin from acorns. Rangers who specialize in Indian interpretation tell the story well.

When use of the California coast developed quickly, after the discovery of gold in 1848, the elephant seals were pushed to the brink of extinction. Hunters slaughtered the large mammals for their skins and their blubber, which was rendered for lamp oil. Seals sleeping fearlessly on the beaches, oblivious to mere 150 to 200-pound humans, were no match for gunpowder weaponry. By 1892 hunters presumed they had exploited the species down to the last animal, but a handful survived on remote Guadalupe Island, off Baja California.

Similarly, the coast suffered from development and exploitation that the citizens of California eventually declared rapacious.

The first enduring settlements—21 Spanish missions built between 1769 and 1831—dotted the coast at fairly regular intervals from San Diego to Sonoma, north of San Francisco. They were often adjacent to a small town and garrison. The Spaniards built them to subjugate the Indians, convert them to Christianity, teach them Spanish and some useful trades, and thereby control the frontier. The system lasted for 65 years, although it did not in the long run accomplish its goal. Many of the missions are now restored and open to visitors.

The rapid rise of San Francisco in 1849 dwarfed the mission communities. In six months over 700 ships anchored in San Francisco harbor so that both passengers and crew could make a dash for the Sierra foothills—and gold. A walk among the small warehouses and shops in the Jackson Square Historic Area of San Francisco gives you some feeling for the red-brick-and-wood city of the 1850s.

Wood to build San Francisco came from entrepreneurs in the redwood country of the north coast. William Carson of Eureka was one of the most successful of these lumber barons. His elegant provincial Victorian house in Eureka offers you a quaint, gingerbread encounter with the 1880s. Carpenter Gothic cottages in nearby Ferndale feature similar charms on a more modest scale.

Los Angeles developed late in the history of coastal California. It remained a quiet Spanish-Mexican pueblo until the late nineteenth and early twentieth century, when imported water, railroad tracks, oil discoveries at Signal Hill, and skilled promotional efforts combined to create a boom. On chilly winter evenings in Minnesota, potential immigrants read promotional pieces that described trees laden profusely with oranges against a background of snowcapped mountains. This enticement still endures east of Riverside on days when air quality permits.

In a recent and hopeful chapter of California coastal history, the fate of the elephant seals also parallels the fortunes of the entire coast.

When the seals and the market for seal oil vanished, the United States and Mexico agreed jointly to protect any remaining members of the species. Gradually the elephant seals at Guadalupe Island increased their numbers and expanded their range. Today the elephant seals have increased to 30,000, enough to remove them from the endangered list. I remember a visit to Ano Nuevo in 1975 to see the first elephant seal born on the U.S. mainland in this century.

In the 1970s Californians voted to save the coast from total destruction. They passed Proposition 20, which declared that the state's 1,100 miles of coastline are a resource to be preserved, protected, and kept accessible "for the enjoyment of the current and the succeeding generations." Translated into workable law, the proposition became the state Coastal Commission, which has ruled on over 35,000 permits since 1973, reconciling the rights of private ownership with the interests of the public. People who treasure the coast believe that the commission's achievements are laudable, and not a moment too soon.

I watched the bull elephant seal fall slowly back to sleep, undisturbed by my presence. Pondering his existence here as 1 individual of 30,000, mine as 1 of 22 million, and the beauty of Ano Nuevo as a microcosm of the entire California coast filled me with a fuller sense of life, a wish that this peaceful coexistence could continue, and a confidence that the balance could be maintained.

*This rocky coastline near Bodega Bay lies fifty miles north of San Francisco in Sonoma County.*

*A twisted old cypress clings to the shore, defying the wind and surf of the rugged Monterey Peninsula.*

Wind, rock, and water shape sandstone along the tideline at Point Lobos State Reserve, south of Carmel.

Overleaf: Pinnacle Rock and the azure Pacific surf typify scenic contrasts at Point Lobos State Reserve.

*Palm trees stand guard over La Jolla Point, north of San Diego, while high tide explodes against the sandstone cliffs below.*

*The prow of "Star of India," a Cape Horner launched in 1863, frames San Diego Bay from her permanent mooring on the waterfront.*

Two surfers harness a massive breaker at Huntington beach, one of the more popular surfing spots in southern California.

*Sailboats catch a late afternoon breeze to traverse the Santa Barbara harbor.*

*The mansions, pools, terraced gardens, exotic trees, and outbuildings of the Hearst Castle sprawl across 123 acres of the Santa Lucia Mountains at San Simeon; they are now a state historical monument open to the public.*

*Although a portion of Mission San Juan Capistrano (built between 1796 and 1806) has been restored, visitors seem most interested in the cliff swallows that return to the ivy covered ruins each spring on St. Joseph's Day.*

*Sunlight filters down through a grove of towering coastal redwoods (Sequoia sempervirens) in Jedediah Smith State Park on the north coast near Crescent City.*

*Redwood tycoon William Carson built this eighteen-room Victorian mansion in Eureka during the 1880s; today it serves as a private club.*

*The Pacific Ocean stretches to the horizon from Mount Tamalpais, the prominent peak just north of the Golden Gate Bridge in Marin County.*

The western span of the Bay Bridge stretches its two decks of multi-laned highway from Yerba Buena Island toward downtown San Francisco.

Large combers have been breaking against this rocky shore since long before Cabrillo sailed past it in 1542 on his way into Monterey Bay.

*The sprawling Los Angeles basin stretches out below the Griffith Park Observatory, with the lights of Hollywood and Santa Monica in the foreground.*

# The Sierra Nevada

Your best guide to the Sierra Nevada of California is a Scotsman who came to California from Wisconsin. His life was a long and joyous ramble through nature. Fortunately for California, he became friends with a horticulturalist in Martinez, a town northeast of San Francisco, and subsequently married the man's daughter. Thus anchored in the Golden State, this erstwhile wanderer spent a decade making a quick fortune in fruit growing and then turned to writing persuasive magazine articles and books about conserving the Sierra of California and wilderness forests throughout the country.

That guide is none other than John Muir, the founding father of the U.S. environmental movement.

Muir walked the whole length of the Sierra and wrote about different areas in his *The Mountains of California*. His writings combined an exuberant feeling for nature, a thorough competence as a botanist, a keen observational eye for natural phenomena, and an apostolic fervor toward preserving the rapidly disappearing wilderness.

As early as the 1880s Muir perceived that forests and scenic areas were undergoing rapid development that would destroy forever their wilderness character. At a time when our richly endowed country consumed its resources profligately, Muir sounded an effective alarm.

"Wilderness is a necessity," he wrote. "Mountain parks and (forest) reservations are useful not only as fountains of timber and irrigating rivers, but as fountains of life."

Muir's first writings helped in the drive to consolidate Yosemite National Park. In 1892 he formed the Sierra Club and served as its president until his death in 1914. On a famous 1903 campout in Yosemite Park, he reinforced Theodore Roosevelt's own conservation ethic. Roosevelt's presidency later included setting aside 23 national monuments, 5 national parks, and national forests covering 148 million acres.

Curl up with one of Muir's books, such as *The Yosemite*, and bask in his sunlight prose, learning much about the song of the water-ouzel, the majesty of the immense *Sequoia gigantea* trees in Wawona Grove, and the delicacy of mountain fritillary butterflies. In Martinez you can visit Muir's house, now a National Historic Site, and immerse yourself in his life-enhancing vision.

For many travelers a first encounter with Yosemite Valley prompts feelings similar to those recorded by one of the soldiers in the Mariposa Battalion, a squad sent in 1851 to locate marauding Indians who had retreated into the unknown valley.

"As I looked," wrote the awestruck man, "a peculiar exalted sensation seemed to fill my whole being, and I found my eyes in tears with emotion."

I remember my own first experience of that "exalted sensation." On a June morning I drove several miles up the narrow mouth of the valley, wondering when I would arrive, for Yosemite's approach is a long prelude rather than an easy presentation of the treasures. Suddenly the stark granite face of El Capitan, clothed in a deep purplish light, rose in front of me across the Merced River. I stopped the car to walk to the edge of the river. Redbud bushes were in flower. Blue lupines crowded each other in the meadow. Set back in the woods, the white blossoms of dogwood showed prominently. I looked up at the 3,464-foot granite monolith, El Capitan. The valley was entirely quiet. Since I had left my car, there was no road immediately apparent, and no other people in sight. Life that day, enlarged by El Capitan, felt full and noble.

I drove and hiked to see all the falls, such as Yosemite Falls, which drops 2,425 feet in a two-tiered plunge. In spring after a normally wet winter all the falls of Yosemite flow, with Bridleveil, the most diaphonous. In winter I've skied at Badger Pass, and in autumn I've walked the valley floor, soft and damp after the first rains, with leaves turning red on the dogwood and yellow on the black oak trees — source of the essential staple for the acorn diet of the Ahwahnee Indians of Yosemite. Shafts of light that steal over the rim of the valley and through the coloring trees sometimes illuminate a single tree brilliantly. In summer Yosemite hosts so many visitors that a traveler fortunate to arrive at other seasons enjoys a better experience.

Two other places I most recommend seeing are Lassen National Park and Lake Tahoe.

Lassen Park, east of Redding, has an adjective in its title: Volcanic. The volcanic presence provided the rationale historically for purchasing the land as a park. Today this vulcanism permeates the terrain, whether it is hot present activity, such as the fumaroles and hot springs at Bumpass Hell, or cold

*Left: In Yosemite Valley, the Merced River plunges 317 feet over Vernal Fall, called "Cloud of White" by the Indians.*

reminders of past eruptions that you can see when you peer into Lassen crater.

Payment for Lassen Park bought for the public more than we bargained for. When the first sections were purchased in 1906, the 10,457-foot Lassen Peak was thought to be the best example of an extinct volcano in the United States. The holdings included a textbook geologic image of a Cinder Cone, symmetrical and 700 feet high, northeast of Lassen Peak. The public's bonus in this purchase occurred on May 30, 1914, when "extinct" proved to be a premature description. On that remarkable Memorial Day a cloud of steam rose from Lassen Peak to usher in 150 spectacular eruptions, a seven-year performance. The greatest show of all occurred on May 19, 1915, when a river of lava poured a thousand feet down the side of the mountain, creating a mud flow a quarter-mile wide and 18 miles long. Three days later a dramatic upheaval known as the Great Hot Blast shot debris five miles into the air and felled pine trees like bowling pins around the base of the mountain. Inches of ash fell on towns as far away as Reno. For northern Californians with a strong religious persuasion and an apocalyptic temperament, this was sufficient evidence that the final days were at hand. But eventually the mountain quieted down.

When you hike in Lassen or drive the excellent Loop Road, you seldom lose sight of Lassen Peak, hovering like a benign deity. The beauty of the mountain for a traveler parallels what Seattleites see in Rainier or the Japanese in Fuji. There is always another view, a different light, to be savored. Closeup from Summit Lake I have seen Lassen wear a pink mantle. Farther away, from Juniper Lake, the peak has looked orange. Motorists on the Loop Road in the park seem to circle the peak, respectfully paying homage, turning at appointed hours of the day, as Moslems bend toward Mecca, honoring this volcanic spirit. John Muir considered the hemlock trees on the south slopes of Lassen the finest examples he had seen of that species.

Alpine Lake Tahoe ranks as another main attraction of the California Sierra because of its impressive altitude, size, depth, and varying colors. The lake rests at 6,228 feet in a huge granite basin fenced by the Sierra on the west and the Carson Range on the east. It stretches 21.6 miles long, and extends 8–12 miles wide, with an average depth of 1,000 feet. Sixty-three tributaries and snowmelt feed the lake. Tahoe's volume of water could provide 50 gallons a day for five years to every American.

Drive the 71-mile shoreline in summer for an exhilarating outing, stopping at the inspiring turnoffs. Tahoe's name came from the word *lake* in the language of the Washoe Indians, who used Tahoe as a summer camp and fishing lake. Tahoe's colors range from deep blue to pale green, depending on the light. Linger at Emerald Bay on the south end of the lake to witness scenic superlatives.

Backpackers head into Desolation Wilderness on the southwest side of the lake. The area entices the hiker in autumn when willows and alders show their color, and eleven ski areas attract visitors in winter. Entrepreneur E. J. "Lucky" Baldwin developed one of the first resorts on the lake. His promotional brochure insisted, "To obtain the air the angels breathe, you must go to Tahoe."

John Muir approached Tahoe with his usual energy, writing in 1878, "I have just returned from a week of bracing weather at Lake Tahoe, in which we enjoyed glorious views of winter, fine rolling and sliding in the snow, swimming in the icy lake, and lusty reviving exercise on snowshoes that kept our pulses dancing right merrily."

Your guide's final advice and best wisdom on the Sierra reads, "Climb the mountains and get their good tidings. Nature's peace will flow into you as sunshine flows into trees, the winds will blow their own freshness into you and the storms their energy, while cares will drop off like autumn leaves."

*Right: A small Sierra stream is a mosaic of ice, snow, and water in the sunshine of a midwinter day.*

*A bristlecone pine, a specimen of the world's oldest known living trees, survives in the Patriarch Grove of the White Mountains, east of Bishop.*

*These tufa pinnacles, formed by the higher water levels of earlier years, show that brackish Mono Lake is slowly dying, as runoff from the eastern slope is diverted to the south.*

*Water cascades from a small lake below the Minarets, in the Ritter Range just east of Yosemite National Park.*

*The Big Trees, or Sequoia gigantea, tower upward to 300 feet and reach diameters of 35 feet across the base, as exemplified by the Senate Group in Sequoia National Park.*

*The glow of a late fall afternoon picks out a canopy of oak leaves and an American elm that some early pioneer planted in Yosemite Valley.*

*From the western entrance to Yosemite Valley, El Capitan and Bridalveil Fall look much the same as they did in 1851 when a militia company stumbled into the valley and returned to publicize its wonders.*

This boulder-strewn Sierra stream is one of hundreds of creeks that converge to form the major rivers that water central California.

*A stream plunges toward Emerald Bay, located on the west side of Lake Tahoe, the twenty-mile-long mountain-ringed "jewel" of the Sierra crest.*

*June Lake, a popular recreation spot, lies in a canyon on the steep eastern slope in Inyo National Forest.*

The snow-capped southern Sierra peaks are seen here from the granite-studded Alabama Hills, near Lone Pine.

Overleaf: Winter's frigid temperatures have frozen Lake Ellery near 9,941 foot Tioga Pass.

*The sheer granite face of Half Dome is a prominent feature in Yosemite Valley, viewed here from Glacier Point with Tenaya Canyon and Clouds Rest in the background.*

The Tuolumne River, in northern Yosemite, springs from the Lyell and McClure glaciers and wanders through Tuolumne Meadows before flowing into Hetch Hetchy Reservoir.

Grand Sentinel is one of several 4,000-foot peaks that rise above Zumwalt Meadows, not far from Cedar Grove in Kings Canyon National Park.

*The transition point of the Sierra Nevada and the Cascade Range is Lassen Peak, a recently active volcano reflected here in tranquil Manzanita Lake.*

*Silver Lake lies at the foot of Carson Peak in a zone of mixed granite and volcanic rock.*

*Giant granite boulders are debris left by powerful glaciers that scoured the Sierra Nevada four successive times during the Pleistocene.*

# The Valleys

I recall my first drive down Interstate Highway 5 in 1972, shortly after the fast, arrow-straight new section opened on the west side of the Central Valley. At the time there were few gas stations and restaurant stops built along the road. At Los Banos I looked out the window eastward and saw fields of almonds and broccoli as far as my eye could penetrate. Then I drove on, and on and on, until my watch told me another hour had elapsed. I looked out again. Crops had changed to alfalfa and peaches, but the same endless stretch of farmlands ranged before and behind me. It seemed that I had made scarcely any progress down the valley.

The Central Valley extends 465 miles from Redding to Bakersfield and stretches 25 to 50 miles wide, consisting of two large watersheds, the Sacramento River and San Joaquin River drainages. This and other valleys of California generate $10 billion annually in agricultural sales, 9 percent of all agricultural income in the United States.

The diversity of California farming owes much to patterns established by the mission fathers, who planted fruit trees and vegetables, as well as raising cattle, sheep, and horses. When the missions disbanded as a result of secularization orders from Mexico in 1832, the inventory of cattle was 151,180 and of sheep, 137,969. Farming expanded rapidly after the gold rush because the miners themselves made a large and hungry market. Completion of the transcontinental railroad in 1869 opened the East to California agricultural products. Wheat soon became a dominant crop, with wheat farmers and the railroad struggling to control the wealth. Frank Norris's novel *The Octopus* portrays the era well.

Today California farmers produce both quantities and varieties of food in record amounts—some 200 major crops, a range that exceeds any other state's agriculture. Sixty-two thousand farms cultivate 33 million acres. As an exporter of food and fiber, California ships out $2 billion worth per year, exceeded only by the grain and soybean giants, Illinois and Iowa. The Orient has been emerging as a major market for California food products. Japan is currently the biggest buyer, but in the 1980s exporters will undoubtedly ship food products to China and other oriental destinations. Refrigerated containers, loaded right in the field, can be trucked to Oakland and sent to the orient on large, swift container ships, with a lapse of only seven days from fields to market.

The grand scale of California agriculture becomes more comprehensible and the diversity more apparent when you drive into small towns and see the billboards: in Castroville, "The Artichoke Capital of the World"; in Salinas, "The Lettuce Capital of America"; in Holtville (Imperial Valley), "The Carrot Capital of the World"; and in Lindsay, "A Nice Town, A Great Olive." Both Half Moon Bay on the coast, and Manteca in the Central Valley, claim to be "The Pumpkin Capital of America."

The wonder of agriculture in California's valleys is that the season never ends. While winter grips most of the country, grapefruit, asparagus, and strawberries are shipped out of Riverside County. When asparagus becomes available from the Central Valley, the southern area has planted lettuce and carrots. Harvests of cauliflower, lettuce, potatoes, and carrots in the Salinas Valley continue year round.

The most romantic agricultural crop of California's valleys is wine grapes, which become 200 million gallons of table wine annually. California produces over 90 percent of all U.S. wine. Grapes are grown in more regions of California than any other crop. Two wine industries flourish side by side. In the hot Central Valley large, lush vines bear a heavy tonnage that makes a competent, everyday wine. The common wines of California are, to my palate, more uniformly drinkable and tasty, as well as a better buy for the consumer, than the common wines I've drunk in Europe. Quality control and technical competence in the California wine industry is high, with many personnel trained in the enology school at the University of California, Davis. The largest volume wineries, such as Gallo (a third of all California wine), United Vintners, Guild, and Franzia have their operations in the Central Valley.

With dry table wine consumption increasing about 12 percent each year in the United States, more buyers are moving to the higher quality wines that come from the cooler coastal valleys, primarily the Napa, Sonoma, and Monterey regions. The most exciting California wine story in the 1980s is the rapid development of Monterey as a prime varietal growing area. In 1962 there were almost no commercial wine grapes growing in Monterey. By 1979 over 34,000 acres had been planted to Riesling, Chardonnay, Cabernet, and Zinfandel, as well as some other top varietals. The fruity white wines of

*Left: A tractor plowing furrows is dwarfed by this giant field in the Central Valley near Los Banos.*

Monterey, Riesling and Chardonnay, get my vote as the best expression of these varieties in California. The reason is partly that Monterey has the longest and coolest growing season of the coastal valleys, approximating the Riesling climate of Germany's Mosel and Rheingau. I would still favor Napa and Sonoma as the best producers of Cabernet or Zinfandel, a grape that does well in California, but whose European origins are obscure.

Tasters who begin exploring California wines will find the range of choices exciting. Small producers have become famous for their quality, such as Santa Clara County's Ridge Winery has for its Cabernet. Some areas not immediately considered wine country have become well known for a specialty — such as Amador in the Gold Country for Zinfandel. While quality and quantity improve, prices are held down by the new competitors entering the marketplace.

The 1970s saw California emerge as a wine producer capable of equaling the best production of Europe's select regions. As an interested wine taster who has sampled the best wines available in Bordeaux, Burgundy, the Mosel, and the Rheingau, I can only say that in the 1980s California wine will shed the last vestige of inferiority that snobbism attaches to our domestic production. This is a tremendous achievement in viticulture when you consider that the entire wine industry was dismantled during Prohibition, which was repealed only in 1933.

Cotton and grapes are the most valuable California crops in dollar sales, but the full range of crops is surprising. Dates are an example. The Coachella Valley east of Palm Springs, centering around Indio, has an intensely dry and hot climate, about 106 degrees average temperature each day in July, second only to Death Valley as the hottest place in the United States. This climate, even warmer than that of Libya, is ideal for dates. Each year about 14,500 tons are harvested from high trees that strike the traveler with their oasis-like aura. The main variety in this $16 million a year business is the semidry Deglet Noor; it accounts for about 90 percent of the commercial crop because it is hard and dry enough for mechanical harvesting and processing, although discriminating users prefer softer varieties, such as Bahri. Indio hosts a National Date Festival at the end of the annual harvest, the third week of February.

The position of agriculture in California's valleys would seem enviable, but three major concerns emerge as we look to the future.

First, there is water input. When the forty-niners crossed the San Joaquin Valley, they called it "the Badlands." Most California agriculture depends on irrigation by water stored in vast reservoirs, with Shasta Lake as the key, and transported by means of canals to the central and southern growing areas. Demand for water increases, straining the system even in wet years. The 1975–1977 drought came within a few months of destroying California agriculture. In the next drought the damage could be even greater.

Second, this agricultural system is energy intensive. Fossil fuels produce fertilizers, run farm machinery, pump in the water, harvest and process the crops, and transport them to distant markets. As the price of fossil fuels soars, costs in the entire system increase dramatically.

Third, pesticide use or abuse, depending on your point of view, jumps each year in California. In 1974 over 56 million pounds of pesticides were used in the state. Four years later the annual figure had doubled to 111 million pounds. As insects become resistant and resurgent, farmers reach for more toxic materials. Pesticides kill predator insects as well as pests, and researchers are constantly documenting both damage to the environment and cancer-related effects in humans.

But agriculture in California's valleys also boasts some hopeful stories. Crop stubble and residues — now burned, creating a hazy sky over areas such as the Sacramento delta in the autumn — may be converted into alcohol fuel. Scientists at the University of California, Davis, working with pilot studies converting rice straw and tree prunings, believe they can save 65 million gallons of imported oil per year by fermenting these vegetative wastes.

*Life-giving water from an irrigation system brings nourishment to a spinach field in the Salinas Valley.*

*An airplane view of the Central Valley's fields and canals gives evidence of the grand scale of this vast agricultural resource.*

*Thousands of acres of table and wine grapes grow in California valleys, with the vineyards of the Napa Valley most famous for wine.*

*Today the American River flows serenely near Coloma, where in 1848 James Marshall discovered gold at Sutter's Mill and started the rush of '49.*

This is one of several 68-foot high tailing wheels built in 1912 at the Kennedy gold mine near Jackson that was capable of handling 500 tons of crushed rock per day.

Overleaf: Thousands of ducks and geese take to the air above Tule Lake Wildlife Refuge, near the California-Oregon border on the Pacific Flyway.

Pinnacles National Monument towers over the rolling oak-covered hills east of the Salinas Valley.

Tidytips bloom in profusion in a pasture in the Santa Ynez Valley, north of Santa Barbara.

*Autumn foliage and evergreens surround the rugged, granite spires that give their name to Castle Crags State Park; near the headwaters of the Sacramento River in northern California.*

*Shasta Dam holds the Sacramento in check, forming spectacular Lake Shasta; on the horizon is 14,162-foot Mount Shasta.*

From the air an interstate highway and aqueduct intersect to form an abstract pattern in the Central Valley, where a network of irrigation canals help make California the nation's most productive agricultural state.

*The California poppy (Eschscholtzia californica) the official state flower, grows profusely on the rolling hills and valleys throughout the state.*

*A small herd of Holstein cows rests in a hillside pasture in Marin County, north of San Francisco.*

*Wild oat grass filters the late afternoon sun in the foothills of the Central Valley.*

# The Deserts

From my feet to the horizon stretched a golden carpet of poppies in all directions. The Mojave Desert had sprung alive again. The state flower unfolded its petals to the sun at dawn, and the usually severe face of the desert landscape radiated a brief flush of youth. I was standing near 160th Street West, along Highway 138, about 14 miles from the center of Lancaster. (Desert cities—Phoenix comes to mind—tend to have "streets" stretch to outlying areas where no urban life exists.) This terrain west of Lancaster offers the most lavish showing of *Eschscholtzia californica* to be found today. Funds have been donated to create a State Poppy Park at 150th Street. The park and a visitor center to interpret desert flora will be completed in the 1980s.

I called ahead to the Lancaster Chamber of Commerce to be assured that the weekend I chose to visit the area was a good flowering time. March and April are the months, but moisture levels and temperature affect timing and showiness of the spring parade, which has vintage years similar to wine production. Across from the chamber, in the lobby of the Essex House Hotel, volunteers familiar with the region's flowers offer good maps and suggest viewing areas. Displayed and identified flowers allowed me to match them against illustrations in my copy of Philip Munz's *California Desert Wildflowers*, the guide I recommend.

I found another splendid viewing site at 170th Street East, a mile from Saddleback Butte State Park. A field of yellow coreopsis, *Coreopsis bigelovii*, began at the roadside and extended to foothills three miles away. The small yellow Compositae-family flowers formed on the desert floor a tightly woven fabric that contrasted with the fluffy gold clusters of the poppy habitat west of Lancaster.

That night my family camped at 2,875-acre Saddleback Butte Park. You should not miss this spot for a day or overnight visit, because Saddleback gives you an unspoiled view of the Mojave or high desert, which extends from 2,000- to 5,000-foot elevations. There is also a low desert, the Colorado, from Palm Springs to the Colorado River. Together these deserts comprise 16 million acres, an area which could hold Massachusetts, Connecticut, and New Hampshire.

Saddleback Butte Park preserves a forest of Joshua trees and their accompanying plant life, such as creosote bush, plus the whole web of animal life from termite to desert spiny lizard to ladderbacked woodpecker. *Forest* is a botanically correct but misleading word to the general reader because the desert growth doesn't fit our usual notion of lush, thick stands of vegetation. The Joshua tree is a large member of the lily family, named by migrating Mormons who felt the tree's outstretched arms pointed their way to the Promised Land, as did the prayerful biblical prophet. Large whitish-green clusters of Joshua flowers were showing during my visit. Since the Joshua tree, *Yucca brevifolia*, has no cambium layer, tree-ring dating to determine age is not possible. But observers conclude that a Joshua grows about one inch a year, so the height of a given tree can give you a rough idea of its lifespan. Joshuas reproduce themselves through root sprouts or seeds. Enterprising desert Indians wove Joshua tree leaves into sandals, cut red strands from the inner bark as design material for baskets, and pulverized the seeds into a flour they ate dry or mixed with water as a mush.

A walk around Saddleback Butte in the spring acquaints you with the full range of desert life. Rangers lead informative hikes. During our visit the plants in bloom included beavertail cactus, with their large red flowers, fiddleneck, and golden cholla. On walks in the park we spotted desert tortoises and Mojave ground squirrels.

Much of the Antelope Valley west of Saddleback Butte has been developed for alfalfa production, some 20,000 acres. Tragically, no pronghorn antelopes have survived. When the railroad lines were built through here in 1876, the numerous antelope were psychologically unable to cross the tracks, which cut between their seasonal foraging grounds. Even when starvation threatened, the pronghorns would not cross the tracks. Starvation and two severe winters killed all the antelopes.

The Mojave can be a severe place to live. Temperatures can vary 40 degrees in eight hours. Winds exceeding 100 miles per hour were recorded in July 1976, when many Joshua trees were blown over.

Three other sites in the California desert reward the visitor. They are Joshua Tree National Monument, Anza-Borrego Desert State Park, and Death Valley.

Joshua Tree National Monument, 150 miles east of Los Angeles, is a transition zone between the high and low deserts. As at Saddleback Butte, the domi-

*Left: This desert floor in southeastern California, covered with treacherous cholla cactus, seems a continent away from the misty redwood groves of the northwest coast.*

nant vegetation is the large yucca known as the Joshua tree. Other, diverse plants can also be seen here, such as Washingtonia palm trees in Lost Palm Canyon. Wildlife is fairly extensive in the higher areas, with kangaroo rats jumping before your flashlight beam at night and secretive bighorn sheep present but seldom seen. An impressive view from 5,185 feet, called the Salton View, gives you a sweeping panorama from 235 feet below sea level at Salton Sea to over 10,000 feet above sea level at San Jacinto Peak.

Anza-Borrego Desert State Park, 60 miles northeast of San Diego, is a 480,000-acre preserve with over 600 miles of unimproved roads for the explorer. The park honors the Spanish explorer and settler, Juan Bautista de Anza, who led an expedition through here in 1774. *Borrego* is the Spanish word for the bighorn sheep that live here. Red blossoms of the spindly ocotillo cactus lead the local spring wildflower show.

Travelers interested in Death Valley National Monument should make special efforts to visit in fall, winter, or spring, not summer, because Death Valley consistently has the hottest recorded temperatures on the earth. In 1913 thermometers rose to 134 degrees. Yet in winter the few springs in Death Valley freeze over. The extremes of temperature have fostered one of nature's remarkable stories of adaptation, that of the desert pupfish, whose habitat you can see at Saratoga Springs. The fish survives in highly saline shallow water, hot and almost dry in summer and cold in winter. In Death Valley you can see the lowest place in the United States, at 282 feet below sea level, a few miles from Badwater, itself 279 feet below sea level. My favorite sight in Death Valley is the wind- and sand-chiseled ravine terrain that spreads out from a promontory known as Zabriskie Point. This setting evokes for me the sere, forbidding, and eternal power of the desert more strongly than any other place.

The deserts of southern California will have a larger role to play in our future than in our recent past.

First, we are beginning to make use of the immense sun power falling on the desert. San Diego County now requires new residences in some areas to have solar hot water heating systems. Technologies to harness the sun for warming water and space, and creating steam to make electricity have received their largest impetus here. Over half of the solar heating installations in the United States can be found in California. At Barstow a $123 million solar electricity plant begins operation in 1981, delivering 10,000 kilowatts of power to 6,000 customers. The process uses the sun's rays, focused on a set of mirrors, to boil water whose steam then turns turbines to make electricity.

A second energy bonus in a desert shrub that grows wild in Southern California, Arizona, Sonora, and Baja California, and produces a waxy oil possessing most of the virtues oil users want. The plant, called the jojoba, grows to 15 feet, lives 230 years, thrives in saline soil and water, and tolerates wide ranges of temperature. The oil has a mild odor, no toxicity, and extreme purity; it is unsaturated, doesn't dry, won't turn rancid, and isn't affected by repeated heating. Demand runs high for jojoba oil in applications ranging from automotive oil to the lubricant put into artificial human hearts. As a special bonus, jojoba oil is chemically identical to the prized oil of sperm whales, a circumstance that may ensure the survival of that species. Enthusiasts claim that one acre of jojoba plants equals 30 whales. Farmers are planting jojoba on ranches extending from the Mexican border to Paso Robles.

Visit the California desert in spring to witness the rejuvenative birth of wildflowers in nature's severest environment. Uncountable billions of seeds force their way out of the ground, as if they were lifting the entire floor of the desert, releasing an energy that dwarfs all fossil fuel or nuclear power. This miracle of the life force, stored in the fertile seed, released by the life-giving rain, nourished by the infinitely powerful rays of the sun, forms the basis of all plant and hence animal existence. This insuppressible life force, when seen in the stark desert, can stir witnesses to emulative miracles of their own.

*Red Rock Canyon on the western edge of the Mojave Desert, lies in the rain shadow of the Sierra Nevada.*

Through sand dunes and desert the All-American Canal transports water for irrigation from the Colorado River to the farmlands of the vast Imperial Valley.

The brilliantly colored flower of the beavertail cactus bursts forth from a flat, spined stem where this succulent stores its water.

Overleaf: Quartz monzonite formations catch the last rays of sunlight and silhouette Joshua trees on the high desert at Joshua Tree National Monument.

The Anza-Borrego Desert State Park spreads across almost a half million acres of rugged and barren landscape ranging in elevation from sea level to 8,000 feet.

These Washingtonia palms line Twentynine Palms Canyon in a remote section of Joshua Tree National Monument.

Overleaf: Mesquite Flat dunes in Death Valley National Monument shift restlessly before the hot wind with the Cottonwood Mountains on the horizon.

Sweltering heat beats down on Twenty Mule Team Canyon in Death Valley National Monument, where temperatures can reach 120-degrees (F) in the summer.

*Eroded siltstone forms a pattern of light and shadow below Zabriskie Point in Death Valley.*

*Springtime blossoms of the yucca plant rise majestically from a base of long, narrow leaves.*